Things to kn

There are a few things which we need to know when it comes to star gazing. When you go through the pages of this book you will see references to the Southern and Northern hemisphere. Here we will explain what these mean.

The Southern Hemisphere is the half (hemisphere) of Earth that is south of the equator. It contains all or parts of five continents (Antarctica, Australia, about 40% of Americas, one third of Africa, and several islands off the continental mainland of Asia), four oceans (Indian Ocean, Atlantic Ocean, Southern Ocean, and Pacific Ocean), New Zealand and most of the Pacific Islands in Oceania.

The land in the Northern Hemisphere consists of all of Europe, North America and Asia, a portion of South America, two-thirds of the African continent and a very small portion of the Australian continent with islands in New Guinea.

Which half do you live in? It's important to know this as sometimes the stars can be seen at certain times in one half of the earth and not the other. Sometimes they might even appear upside down depending where you are! Also, just like the Sun and the Moon, constellations also move from East to West

There are some constellations and stars which can be easily seen and used to navigate where other constellations are. One of these is Polaris, which a lot of people refer to as the North star. This star is very easy to spot in the sky on a clear night, even in cities where there is a lot of light pollution. And another is Orion, he is very easy to find by his belt. His belt can be seen as three stars in a line. Once you find these constellations and know where they are, it makes it easier to find other constellations, which sometimes are harder to see, as we can use these as navigational tools to find the others.

Further to these, there are also two more. These are called the big dipper and the little dipper. The North star is part of the little dipper. A lot of people also use these two constellations to navigate their way to others, so these are important constellations to learn also.

It is also important to know how to find the ecliptic line. This is an imaginary line in the sky that marks the annual path of the sun. It is the projection of Earth's orbit onto the celestial sphere. And it is an essential part of any stargazer's vocabulary. The problem with this method is that it requires a bit of time and patience if you want to do it without any tools like a star map. The upside is that you will be able to find any of the zodiac constellations with the same method so you get a 12 by 1 deal.

Below you will learn how to find these constellations, Important stars and how to trace the ecliptic line, along with other constellations. If it's a clear night tonight, have a look outside to see if you can see them.

Ecliptic Line

The ecliptic is an imaginary line in the sky that marks the annual path of the sun. It is the projection of Earth's orbit onto the celestial sphere. It is an essential part of any stargazer's vocabulary. The ecliptic line traces the sun's path in the sky.
The signs of the Zodiac come from the constellations that lie along this line. You can see the ecliptic yourself by drawing a line connecting the planets and the moon.

The ecliptic line directly passes through 13 constellations: Aries, Taurus, Gemini, Cancer, Leo, Virgo, Libra, Scorpius, Ophiuchus, Sagittarius, Capricornus, Aquarius and Pisces. It also passes within a hair's-breath of the constellation of Cetus. Zodiac constellations sit behind the path taken by the Sun as seen from Earth.

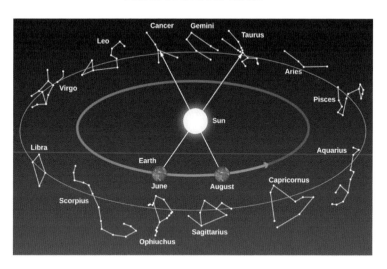

During sunset, look in the direction where the Sun is setting. This is West(ish). Right above the Sun, you will see a bright dot that looks like a star, this is actually Venus. Note its position. Look to the other side, to where the Moon is rising. This is East(ish). Draw an imaginary line between the Moon and Venus. That line is very close to being the exact ecliptic line. If it's about two hours after sunset, you can still trace the ecliptic line, but it might be harder during certain months. Look for a rising slightly red dot in the East. That is Mars. Trace a line between Mars and the Moon and extend it all across the sky. That is the ecliptic plane.

Orion - The Hunter

Orion is very easy to see. As long as it is a clear night you should have no problem finding it. The Constellation Orion is a large bold hunter, standing in the sky with his arm raised, ready to slay any creature that comes close to him!
In the northern hemisphere, the Hunter stands upright. in the southern hemisphere, the Hunter stands upside-down.
You can form his body by finding the famous three stars that make up his belt.

Here is a closer look, can you see these 3 stars in the sky? This is Orion's belt and next to it is the full constellation.

Legends

While hunting on Crete, Orion boasted that he could kill any animal on Earth. Gaia took offence and cracked the earth open, from which a scorpion emerged to kill Orion. Zeus put Orion into the sky, but found it fitting to put the scorpion in the sky as well. To this day, it is said that Orion is still running from the beast that killed him with its deadly sting. This is why you will never see them in the sky at the same time.

Polaris - The North Star

Most people think of the North Star (Polaris) as being the brightest star in the sky, but there are actually many stars much brighter. It is the only star in the sky which does not move and will stay in the same place. However, the North Star does move. It moves in a small circle around the north celestial pole each day but from earth, it looks stationary. The reason Polaris is so important is because the axis of Earth is pointed almost directly at it, meaning Polaris does not rise or set, but remains in almost the same spot above the northern horizon all year, while the other stars circle around it. This means that in the Northern Hemisphere Polaris is relatively easy to find in a northerly direction.

Polaris is part of the constellation of Ursa Minor, also known as Little Bear or Little Dipper. Polaris lies at the end of the handle of the Little Dipper, and is by far the brightest of the 7 stars.

 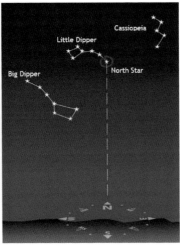

Legends

Long ago, when the world was young, the People of the Sky were so restless and traveled so much that they made trails in the heavens. Now, if we watch the sky all through the night, we can see which way they go.

But one star does not travel. That is the North Star. He cannot travel. He cannot move. When he was on the earth long, long ago, he was known as Na-gah, the mountain sheep, the son of Shinoh. He was brave, daring, sure-footed, and courageous. His father was so proud of him and loved him so much that he put large earrings on the sides of his head and made him look dignified, important, and commanding. Every day, Na-gah was climbing, climbing, climbing. He hunted for the roughest and the highest mountains to climb them.

Once day he found a very high peak. Its sides were steep and smooth, and its sharp peak reached up into the clouds.

Na-gah looked up and said, "I wonder what is up there. I will climb to the very highest point."
Around and around the mountain he traveled, looking for a trail. But he couldn't find one. There was nothing but sheer cliffs all the way around. This was the first mountain Na-gah had ever seen that he could not climb.

He wondered and wondered what he should do. He felt sure that his father would feel ashamed of him if he knew that there was a mountain that his son could not climb.
Na-gah was determined that he would find a way up to the top. His father would be proud to see him standing on the top of such a peak.

Again and again he walked around the mountain, stopping now and then to peer up the steep cliff, hoping to see a crevice on which he could find footing.

Again and again, he went up as far as he could, but always had to turn around and come down.
At last he found a big crack in a rock that went down, not up. Down he went into it and soon found a hole that turned upward. He started to climb up it.

Soon it became so dark that he could not see, and the cave was full of loose rocks that slipped under his feet and rolled down. Soon he heard a big, fearsome noise coming up through the shaft at the same time the rolling rocks were dashed to pieces at the bottom.

.

In the darkness he slipped often and skinned his knees. His courage and determination began to fail. He had never before seen a place so dark and dangerous. He was afraid, and he was also very tired

"I will go back and look again for a better place to climb," he said to himself. "I am not afraid out on the open cliffs, but this dark hole fills me with fear. I'm scared! I want to get out of here!"
But when Na-gah turned to go down, he found that the rolling rocks had closed the cave below him. He could not get down. He saw only one thing now that he could do: He must go on climbing until he came out somewhere.

After a long climb, he saw a little light, and he knew that he was coming out of the hole.
"Now I am happy," he said aloud. "I am glad that I really came up through that dark hole."
Looking around him, he became almost breathless, for he found that he was on the top of a very high peak! There was scarcely room for him to turn around, and looking down from this height made him dizzy. He saw great cliffs below him, in every direction, and saw only a small place in which he could move. Nowhere on the outside could he get down, and the cave was closed on the inside..,
"Here I must stay until I die," he said. "But I have climbed my mountain! I have climbed my mountain at last!

He ate a little grass and drank a little water that he found in the holes in the rocks. Then he felt better. He was higher than any mountain he could see and he could look down on the Earth, far below him.

About this time, his father was out walking over the sky. He looked everywhere for his son, but could not find him. He called loudly, "Na-gah! Na-gah!"

And his son answered him from the top of the highest cliffs. When Shinoh saw him there, he felt sorrowful, to himself, "My brave son can never come down. Always he must stay on the top of the highest mountain. He can travel and climb no more. I will not let my brave son die. I will turn him into a star, and he can stand there and shine where everyone can see him. He shall be a guide mark for all the living things on the Earth or in the sky."
And so Na-gah became a star that every living thing can see. It is the only star that will always be found at the same place.

Always he stands still. Directions are set by him. Travelers, looking up at him, can always find their way.
He does not move around as the other stars do, and so he is called "the Fixed Star." And because he is in the true north all the time, our people call him Qui-am-i Wintook Poot-see. These words mean the North Star.

Besides Na-gah, other mountain sheep are in the sky. They are called "Big Dipper" and "Little Dipper." They too have found the great mountain and have been challenged by it. They have seen Na-gah standing on its top, and they want to go on up to him.

Shinoh, the father of North Star, turned them into stars, and you may see them in the sky at the foot of the big mountain. Always they are traveling. They go around and around the mountain, seeking the trail that leads upward to Na-gah, who stands on the top. He is still the North Star.

Big Dipper

The Big Dipper can be found underneath the little dipper, slightly to the left, which holds the north star. It looks a bit like a frying pan! It is sometimes called the Great Bear. The Big Dipper is one of the largest and most recognizable asterisms in the night sky.

This asterism is located in the northern hemisphere, and it never sets below the horizon. The even bright stars that form the Big Dipper are named, Dubhe, Merak, Phecda, Alioth, Megrez, Mizar, and Alkaid. In the United Kingdom, this asterism is mostly known as the Plough. The Big Dipper gained a lot of attention during ancient times, and it is known throughout the world under many names.

The Big Dipper is formed out of seven bright stars that are shaped like a plough or like an irregular kite. Since the asterism is continually rotating around the North Star, you will see it in different positions throughout the year.

During autumn and winter, the Big Dipper will set closer to the horizon, while in spring and summer, it will be higher in the sky, and it will also appear upside-down. The rule is simple and easy to remember: fall down and spring up. The Big Dipper is not actually an official constellation and is in fact just part of the Ursa Major constellation, but it is very commonly known due to its particular shape, and it can be found in the northern hemisphere

Many confuse the asterism with the whole constellation of Ursa Major. However, Ursa Major has many more stars

One of the stars in the Big Dipper, namely Alkaid, was believed to have magical properties during the medieval age.

Its brightest star, Alioth, is 102 times brighter than the Sun, with a magnitude of 1.8. Dubhe is Big Dipper's second brightest star, with a magnitude of 1.8. It is found 124 light-years away, and it 316 times more luminous than our Sun.

Dubhe and Merak form the Pointer, a line which is used to find Polaris, the North Star.

The Big Dipper gained a lot of attention during ancient times, and it is known throughout the world under many names.

The Big Dipper is among the most famous asterisms in the night sky. The ancients knew about it, and many civilizations attributed great significance to it.

Legends

In South Korean mythology, The Big Dipper is also called "The seven stars of the north." It is said that a widow, along with her seven sons, used to go by the house of a widower, but to get there, they had to cross a river. Each son places a stone into the water so that it would be easier to get to the other side. The mother didn't know who put the stepping stones there, so she blessed them, and when her sons died, they became the constellation.

According to a Native American legend, the Big Dipper bowl is a bear, and the three stars that form the handle are three hunters trying to capture the bear. In another interpretation, the handle represents three cubs that follow their mother.

In an Arabian story, the Big Dipper bowl illustrates a coffin, and the three stars of the handle, Alkaid, Mizar, and Alioth, are mourners who follow the casket.

The Big Dipper was known among the slaves in the United States as the "Drinking Gourd." They used it to find north and to follow their path to freedom. Similarly, the asterism was used by the Jews who were escaping the concentration camps during World War II.

According to legend, Ursa Major, which both the Big Dipper and the Little dipper are part of, was once the beautiful maiden Callisto, whom the god Zeus had an affair with. In order to protect her and their son, Arcas, from his jealous wife Hera, Zeus turned Callisto and Arcas into bears. He then picked up the bears by their short, stubby tails and threw them into the sky.

There is a beautiful Native American legend which tells a story of a group of hunters who got lost in the forest. They prayed to the spirits to send them help to find their way home. Suddenly a small girl appeared to the hunters and said she was the spirit of the pole star. She led them home. Polaris was known as the star that does not move. When they died the hunters were placed into the sky where they forever follow the pole star.

Little Dipper

The Little Dipper is an asterism that belongs to the constellation of Ursa Minor. It consists of seven stars, the most important one being Polaris, also known as the North Star.

There are seven stars that form the Little Dipper asterism, and they are Kochab, Urodelus, Yildun, Polaris, Pherkad, Ahfa al Farkadain and Anwar al Farkadain. Polaris is the brightest star of this asterism and the current North Star, revealing the North Celestial Pole's location.

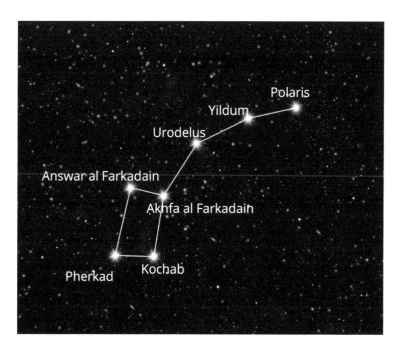

The little Dipper, and the Big Dipper, are part of the Ursa Major Constellation.

Legends

To most observers the constellation of Ursa Minor is better known as the Little Dipper. In mythology Ursa Minor is Arcas, the son of Zeus and the maiden Callisto (Ursa Major). Arcas and Callisto were changed into bears and placed in the sky by Zeus in order to be protected from his jealous wife Hera.

Boötes Constellation

Boötes is one of the largest constellations in the sky. Located in the northern celestial hemisphere, the constellation is dominated by the Kite, a diamond-shaped asterism formed by its brightest stars. Boötes is the 13th largest constellation in the night sky. Arcturus is a red giant star an is the brightest star in the constellation Boötes. Arcturus is also among the brightest stars that can be seen from Earth.

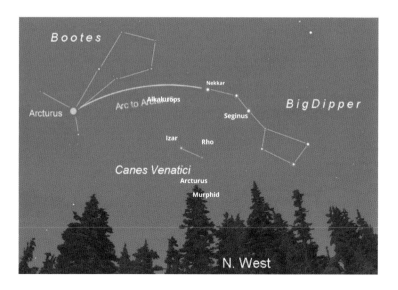

Legends

Some say that Boötes is the most ancient constellation in the sky. Indeed, it has been recognised by numerous cultures in slightly different forms. Even the Greeks were not clear on its history. The first reference to the name Boötes comes from "The Odyssey" by Homer almost three Millenia ago.

In one of his most popular incarnations, he is called the Hunter and, with his Hounds, he eternally circles the Bears, Ursa Major and Ursa Minor, around the North Pole. In fact, the brightest star in Boötes is Arcturus, which can be loosely translated as "Bear Guard."

He is also called the Herdsman and his journey around the pole represents his task of keeping the celestial beasts together.

Another legend says that Bootes was the son of Zeus and Callisto. Hera changed Callisto into a bear who was almost killed by Boötes when he was out hunting. Luckily, he was rescued by Zeus and he took him into the sky where she is now Ursa Major, the Great Bear.

Yet another myth says that he was the son of Demeter, the goddess of agriculture. Supposedly he was given a place in the sky for inventing the plow.

Hercules - Son Of Zeus

The Hercules constellation is a lopsided-shaped boxy pattern of stars located in the skies of the northern hemisphere. It's visible in the evening skies from early March to late September each year and appears directly overhead at midnight in June. As one of the earliest constellations to be observed, Hercules has a rich history. Observers in the northern hemisphere should have no problem finding Hercules. For star gazers in the southern hemisphere, it appears much farther north in the sky for individuals as far south as the tip of South America. You can find Hercules between two brilliant stars: Arcturus and Vega.

When can Hercules be seen?

Hercules is one of the largest constellations in the night sky but doesn't contain any very bright stars.
The constellation is visible in both the Northern and Southern hemispheres.
In the Northern hemisphere Hercules can be seen from April to November.
In the Southern hemisphere Hercules can be viewed from June to September.
In the Southern hemisphere Hercules will appear upside down.

Legends

Hercules lived the majority of his life in splendor, displaying his superior powers very early on. His strength was made clear when he destroyed two snakes before they could strike, which had silently crawled into the crib where he and his twin baby brother Iphikles (IH-fih-kleez) slept . What no one knew at that time was that Hera (HAYR-UH), the wife of Zeus and the children's step mother, was the one who made certain those snakes got into the crib in the first place.

It was Hera's jealousy and bitter need for revenge that would define most of Hercules' life from his birth on, as well as the struggles he would endure throughout his entire life. Why was Hera's rage aimed at such a young and special child? This will become all too clear as we discover the many trials in the life of Hercules. When the news reached Hera that the snakes were destroyed, thus foiling her plan to kill the baby Hercules, she immediately devised a new plan. You see, Hera was the wife of Zeus at that time, who came to discover Zeus had tricked Alcmene—Hercules' mother, who's beauty Zeus could not resist—into having an affair by disguising himself as her husband who had been away on business for many years. When their child was born, Alceme named the baby boy Hercules, which meant "Hera's glorious gift". As you can imagine, this just made the goddess Hera more angry and extremely jealous! It was at that moment Hera swore revenge. She set out to make the life of this child as horrible as possible. She bitterly, yet patiently plotted her revenge and would wait to make her move at just the right time...

Before Hercules had turned eighteen years old—when most Greek boys were considered men—he had an arsenal of superior weapons and war materials that had been graciously given to him by some of the most powerful of gods. These weapons consisted of a mighty bow and arrows, a powerful club, an indestructible sword, a very special breastplate that was golden, strong horses with great stamina, and a perfect robe to cloak his body beneath. With his grand weapons and powerful beasts, Hercules was prepared to face anything or any enemy that he would encounter throughout his life. But, not even his superior strength, cash of knowledge, and mighty weapons could prepare him for the miserable fate to come; which Hera patiently waited to reign down upon his life.

He had been happily married to Megara (mee-Gayr-uh) for many years ever since her father gave her to the strong man in gratitude for Hercules' good works. This was a common theme in the muscular man's life, as he always helped people wherever he traveled and would fight frequently for good. The two were very happy together and bore many children over the years. Megara's hero husband would prove time and time again just how good of a man he was to his family, as well as all those who knew the powerful man. But, as she had sworn to herself those many years ago, Hera would pop back into Hercules' life to follow through with her deadly plan for revenge.

The goddess Hera finally knew that the time was right to throw her devastating blow of revenge at Hercules. It was then that she cast her staggering spell on Hercules. Such a horrible spell would cause him to spiral into a vicious rage which he had no control over. He did not know what he was doing while in such a fit and unwittingly brutally murdered his wife and all of their children. Once the spell was over, he saw what horrible things he done to his family. He fell to his knees and was certain he would die as well from the pain of such a great disaster. He knew he could not be around people again until he had purged himself of such awful sin. He recognized that he must travel to Delphi, where the most wise of all lived and used the female Oracle to define events that would please the gods.Once in the presence of The Oracle of Delphi, Hercules was told he must serve Eurystheus (yoo-RIS-thee-us), who was a king known to be a coward, as well as very cruel. He would have to serve him for twelve years, where twelve tasks of the kings choosing must be completed. Once these things were done, Hercules would not only find his soul scrubbed clean again, but he would become an immortal for all time. What Hercules would soon discover was that each of these tasks were chosen because of their impossible nature, with most consisting of facing monsters and vicious beasts. Once all twelve task were completed, Hercules was freed from his sinful past and given the gift of immortality. His father, the god Zeus, would take Hercules' life bringing him into the heavens. Hera put down her revengeful ways, and forgave the now immortal muscle man. As a sign of her forgiveness, she gave Hercules her daughter as his bride to live with for eternity, and so he did.

The 12 tasks of Hercules

Here is a list of the 12 tasks Hercules had to complete.

1. Hercules Had to Slay The Nemean Lion - The huge man-eating Nemean lion who had an immortal head and hide that could not be penetrated. Hercules defeated the lion by using his wrestling skills; placing a tight grip around its neck from behind until the lion died from lack of breath. Hercules took the lion's head and hide to wear as his own, he could only skin the beast by using its own sharp claws, as its hide was far too strong to be cut by anything man could create.

2. Hercules Must Defeat Hydra - A fiercely powerful man-eating creature related to Typhon, who has nine heads, with one being secretly immortal. Hydra resides in the stinky swamps where it only comes out to feed. As Hercules would cut off one of its heads, two more would grow back. So, with help of his twin brother, when Hercules cut off one, his brother would sear the wound closed using a fiery torch so it could not grow back. This even worked on the immortal head until the Hyrda was defeated and laying dead on the ground.

3.Hercules Had to Catch a Golden Hind - This task doesn't sound too dangerous as a Hind is only a small fast moving deer. Where the danger resided was in the fact that these creatures were sacred to the goddess Artemis. By catching one, Hercules was just asking for trouble.

4. Hercules Must Chase Down a Deadly Erymanthian Boar - A large b with long sharp tusks was stalking and wounding many of the villagers Arcadia. Hercules was put to task to bring this reign of death to an end. chased down the boar stabbing it with his spear. The swine fell into sor snow where a net was soon cast over him. Hercules swept up the beas the net and carried it back to King Eurystheus.

5. Hercules Had to Clean the Augean Horse Stables in a Single Day - This task was more a test of humility rather than designed to impress. The Augean stables were full of beautiful healthy immortal horses, who made a tremendous amount of manure over the years which had never been cleaned up. In fact, these stables had not been cleaned in over thirty years, and Hercules had to get them clean in a single day. Impossible for most, but not for the man made of muscles as well as brains. He simple rerouted the Alpheus and Peneus rivers to wash away the disgusting mess in a single day.

6. Slay the Stymphalian Birds - Next, Hercules was sent to kill the Stymphallian Birds of prey, which had beaks of bronze and sharp feathers of metal they could shoot at enemies. These birds produced a toxic dung that killed crops, and poisoned the livestock and villagers of Arcadia. Lake Stymphalian was on the edges of Arcadia and is where the birds quickly took over. They roosted deep in the surrounding swamp so Hercules found his muscular body far too heavy for the gooey swamp floor to support. When the goddess Athena noticed what was happening, she gave Hercules a giant rattle to scare the birds from their perch. When the rattle caused the birds to take flight, Hercules was able to shoot most of them with his bow and arrows. This caused the rest of the flock to leave and never return to Arcadia

7. Hercules Must Capture the Cretan Bull - Hercules had to sail to Crete to capture the Cretan Bull. This huge bovine had been uprooting crops and knocking down walls, and simply causing too much damage and trouble. Hercules was to capture the bull and return it to King Eurystheus so he could sacrificed it to Hera. Hercules snuck up on the big brute from behind and subdued it with his strong hands around its neck. He shipped it back to the cowardly King, where Hera denied the sacrifice because she didn't want any glory to fall to Hercules. The bull was put out to pasture and later scarified to Athena (and/or Apollo).

8. Hercules Must Steal the Mares of Diomedes - These mares were crazy and very uncontrollable due to their diet of human flesh, so they had to be tethered to a bronze manger as protection. When Hercules and his helpers came upon these man-eaters he knew he would have to fight the owner, Diomedes, before taking care of the horses. To do this he left his most loved companion Abderus in charge while he went to battle Diomedes. Upon his return Hercules discovered that his companion had been eaten while he was away. In revenge, he fed Diomedes' flesh to mares. After feeding the mares would always become calm. When they finished eating their owner, they were calm enough for Hercules to simply bind their mouths safely shut.

9. Hercules Had to Get the Girdle of Hippolyta - The cowardly king Eurystheus had a daughter who wanted the belt of Queen Hyppolyta, which was a gift from the god of war, Ares. Hyppolyta reigned over the tribe known as the Amazon Warrior Women. The king sent Hercules to get the gift for his daughter. With a group of friends, the powerful man set out to Themiscyra, which was where Hyppolyta lived. It was a hard journey full of fighting and sadness, but Hercules was able to overcome these struggles. When he arrived, Hyppolyta was impressed with such success that she agreed to simply give him the belt. But, Hera had other plans. The revengeful woman took up a disguise and told the villagers that Hercules and his men were there to kidnap the Amazon queen. Worried about their queen, the women rode to Hercules on horseback to see what his intentions truly were. When He saw the warrior women approaching so suddenly and with anger in their eyes, he thought Hippolyta had planned to kill him all along. He knew right then he must kill the queen. Once the queen was dead, Hercules took the belt from her and delivered it back to Eurythesus and his spoiled daughter.

10. Hercules Had to Get the Cattle of the Monster Geryon - In this task, Hercules had to travel to the Mediterranean island of Erytheia to round up the cattle. It would seem a simple labor, but Hera sent a biting fly (gladfly) to nip the cattle causing them to become irritated and thus spread out as they ran from the biting nuisances. They spread out so far that it took Hercules a full year to round them all up. Hera then flooded the river so it was impossible for him to get the cattle across without drowning.

But, this did not stop the strong man, he made a bridge of stones that made the river shallow. This made it safe to cross the herd and complete his task by delivering the cattle to the court of Eurystheus, where upon their arrival the herd was sacrificed to Hera.

11. Hercules Had to steal the Apples of Hesperides - When Hercules made it to the garden of Hesperides, he tricked Atlas into stealing some of the apples for him. Because Atlas was related to Hesperides it would not seem so unlikely that he took some apples, making this task much easier for the strong man than any other so far.

12. Hercules Had to Capture and Bring Back Cerberus - Not only was this labor his last, but it was the most difficult. To accomplish the task, he would first have to learn how to get in and out of the underworld alive, where Cerberus—the three-headed guardian hound of the underworld—could be found. To do this, he went to Eleusis and learned the Eleusinian Mysteries. Once in the underworld, Hercules located Hades (the god of the underworld) asking if he could have permission to take Cerberus to the surface. Hades agreed to allow this task, but only if Hercules was able to defeat the three-headed beast without using a single weapon. Hercules was able to beat the beast with his powerful muscles, carrying it out of the underworld over one shoulder. When he presented the beast, the cowardly king was so scared that he begged Hercules to take it back to the underworld. Once he had completed this deed the king would release him from his labors. So Hercules took the beast back to its place at the gates of the underworld.

Pegasus - The Flying Horse

Pegasus is best spotted on dark nights beginning in late September and early October. It's not far from W-shaped Cassiopeia and lies just above Aquarius. Cygnus the Swan is not too far away, either. Look for a group of stars in the shape of a box, with several lines of stars extending out from the corners

When can Pegasus be seen?

Pegasus is visible in both the Northern and Southern hemispheres. In the Northern hemisphere Pegasus can be seen from July to January. In the Southern hemisphere the constellation can be viewed from August to December. In the Southern hemisphere Pegasus will appear upside down

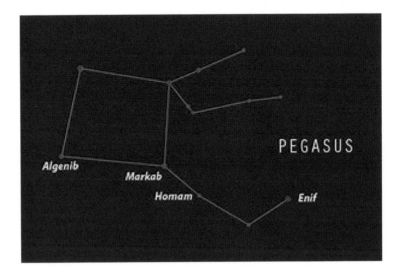

Legends

Pegasus was an immortal winged horse, one of the two children of Poseidon and Medusa. Along with his brother, the golden-sworded Chrysaor, Pegasus sprang forth most miraculously from his pregnant mother's neck after Perseaus, who was a greek hero and slayer of monsters, beheaded her.
Pegasus was wild at first and is one of the most famous magical creatures in mythology. The beautiful winged horse was a favorite subject of Greek artists and continues to be an often-used form today.
The flying horse is arguably more famous today than the hero who tamed him. Bellerophon is the mans name who tamed Pegasus.
Bellerophon appealed to Athena and Poseidon, both gods associated with horses and equestrian inventions, to obtain a bridle that would tame Pegasus.
Following Polyidus's instructions, Bellerophon found Pegasus drinking at the Pirene spring outside of Corinth. When the hero slipped Athena's magical bridle onto the horse, it followed his instructions and allowed him to mount it.
Pegasus flew his first rider to confront the Chimera, who was a monster he wanted to kill. The flying horse's great speed and agility saved Bellerophon from being engulfed by the monster's fiery breath. Bellerophon shot arrows at the monster, but none could penetrate its skin. He urged Pegasus into a daring dive to ram his lead-tipped spear into the Chimer's throat instead. Unable to breathe out its flames, the Chimera was burned from within and died. The speed of Pegasus had allowed Bellerophon to complete his impossible quest.
The flying horse aided Bellerophon in many later adventures as well. Striking from far above, the hero was able to out maneuver and ambush any enemies he faced.

Eventually, however, Pegasus would play a role in Bellerophon's downfall. After many great victories, the hero became convinced that he had earned a place among the gods and he urged his horse to fly to Mount Olympus. There are several different stories about what happened to Bellerophon when he tried to ride Pegasus to Olympus. According to one, Zeus was so angered by the mortal's arrogance that he sent a gadfly to sting Pegasus on the back. Like any horse, Pegasus bucked and reared when he was stung. Bellerophon was thrown from its back. Injured in the fall, he lived the rest of his life disabled and alone.
Other stories say that the hero became filled with doubt as he neared Olympus, believing it was not really the home of the gods. When he looked down at the earth below him he lost his grip and fell to his death, his lack of faith preventing him from becoming a god.

Although Pegasus is often seen as Hercules loyal horse, Pegasus in fact never served Heracles in classical mythology

Andromeda - The kings daughter

To find constellation Andromeda, first look for the W-shaped constellation Cassiopeia in the northern part of the sky. Andromeda is located directly next to Cassiopeia, and is also connected to a boxy shape of stars that make up the constellation Pegasus.

When can Andromeda be seen?

Andromeda is visible in both the Northern and Southern hemispheres. In the Northern hemisphere Andromeda can be seen from August to February. In the Southern hemisphere the constellation can be viewed from October to December.

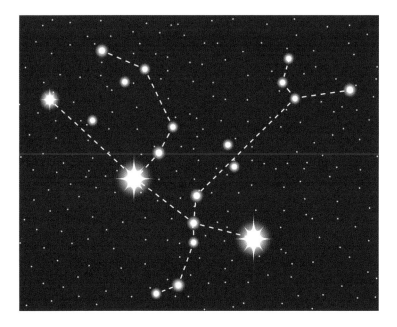

Legends

Andromeda was the daughter of a king, but she was not spoiled at all. Andromeda was as kind as she was beautiful. She was even more beautiful than her mother, the lovely Cassiopeia. Andromeda lived in a city by the sea. She was very happy. Everything was going along swimmingly until one day Andromeda's mother went too far with her boasting.

Her mother boasted about Andromeda all the time. Her mother insisted she was the most beautiful child ever born, except for Aphrodite, of course. One day, she boasted that Andromeda was more beautiful than any of the gods' daughters (except for Aphrodite, of course.)

The trouble started when someone told the Nereids what she had boasted. The Nereids were the daughters of the sea god, Poseidon. Poseidon told his daughters all the time that they were more beautiful than seashells. Who could possibly be more beautiful than seashells? (Except perhaps for Aphrodite.) They whined to their father about it, and whined and whined until Poseidon, in a fit of rage, flooded the city by the sea, and sent a huge sea serpent to devour the entire population, thinking that would certainly shut his daughters up.

The people were terrified. The flood had caused great discomfort. Even after the flood waters receded, the monster kept nipping at people. You never knew when he was going to pop up. He had not eaten anyone yet, but he kept trying. The people were very unhappy.

The king asked a local oracle what he could do to put a stop to things. The oracle told him he had to sacrifice his beloved daughter, Andromeda, if he wanted to save his city. It saddened him greatly, but the king ordered his daughter to be chained to a tree on a cliff that overlooked the sea.

That day, the hero Perseus was out adventuring. He sailed past just as the king's servants were chaining the terrified Andromeda to a tree at the edge of a cliff. Perseus fell in love immediately. As soon as the servants left, Perseus rescued Andromeda, using his magic sickle to cut the chains.

Just then, the giant sea serpent reared its ugly head and reached for Andromeda. Andromeda screamed. Perseus, who was still holding his magic sickle, chopped off the serpent's head.

Naturally, after that, Andromeda loved Perseus as much as he loved her. Perseus wanted her to sail away with him immediately. But Andromeda was insistent that he first ask her father's permission to marry him. She would not feel right about marrying anyone without it.

Perseus offered the king a deal. If the king would let him marry his daughter, Perseus promised to chop off the sea monster's head. The king thought it a very good joke when he heard that Perseus had already killed the monster. When he heard that Perseus' mother was a princess in the famous and rich city-state of Argos, he was even more pleased. When he heard that Perseus' was half god, and his father was the mighty Zeus, the king of all the gods, the king gladly agreed to the wedding.

After the wedding festivities, Perseus sailed away with Andromeda. They headed for his home in the city-state of Argos, where they lived happily ever after.

Cassiopeia - The Queen

Find the "W" shaped stars in the North. (In your side, W may be inverted to M)
Then recognize Ursa Major (the Big Dipper).
Find the two stars at Dipper's edge, which point toward Polaris (the North Star).
Follow the line between two Dippers and the North Star
You will find Cassiopeia on North Star's other side

Cassiopeia constellations

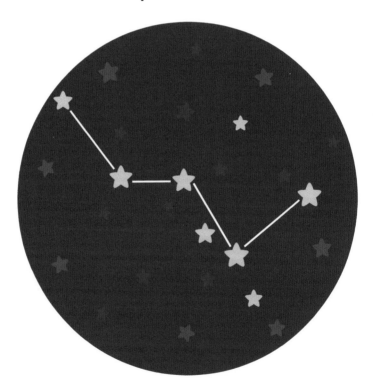

When can Cassiopeia be seen?

Cassiopeia is visible all year in the Northern hemisphere. The constellation is visible in some northerly regions of the Southern hemisphere in late spring

From January to March the constellation will first appear almost overhead around 6 pm, as the evening progresses it will head down towards the horizon in a north-westerly direction, by early morning Cassiopeia will be low on the horizon in a more northerly or north-easterly direction.

From April to June Cassiopeia will be visible low on the horizon in a northerly or north-westerly direction at around 9 pm, moving eastwards it will stay quite low in the sky for several hours before beginning to rise higher around 2 am.

From July to September the constellation will be visible from around 10 pm in a northerly or north-easterly position, as the night progresses it will end up almost directly overhead before day breaks.

From October to December it will appear high in the sky in the north-east at around 6 pm, within a few hours the constellation will move overhead before dipping back down towards the horizon in a north-westerly direction

In the Southern hemisphere the best time to view Cassiopeia is in November and December although the constellation will be low on the horizon, it will first appear around 10 pm in a northerly direction and be visible for a few hours as it heads westwards before dipping below the horizon between 1 and 3 am.

Legends

Cassiopeia was a queen from Greek mythology whose legendary vanity and arrogance ultimately led to her downfall. Cassiopeia was the wife of King Cepheus of Aethiopia and mother to the beautiful Princess Andromeda. One day Cassiopeia proclaimed to the Nereids, female spirits of the sea famed for their beauty, that both she and her daughter were more beautiful and radiant than any of them.

The Nereids passed on their displeasure at Cassiopeia's vain comments to the sea god Poseidon who immediately dispatched a sea monster to destroy Aethiopia. Shocked at the attack Cepheus consulted an oracle who advised him that the only way to appease Poseidon was to sacrifice their daughter. Cepheus and Cassiopeia accepted the advice and chained their daughter to a rock as an offering to the sea monster, luckily for Andromeda she was rescued by the hero Perseus. As an alternative punishment Poseidon sent Cassiopeia into the heavens, spinning around on her throne for eternity.

Cygnus - The Swan

Cygnus is a beautiful constellation that is fairly easy to spot in the night sky, especially if you are far from light pollution. The best way to locate it is by finding five stars in a cross shape, called the Northern Cross, that make up its bulk, which run through the Milky Way. One good indication that you are looking at Cygnus is to search for the bright star Deneb, which sits at the swan's tail and whose name comes from an Arabic word meaning "tail".

Cygnus Constellation

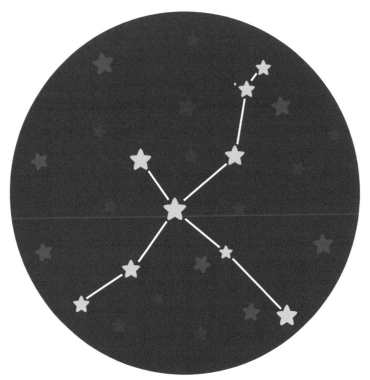

When can Cygnus be seen?

For those in the Northern Hemisphere, during June and July, Cygnus can be seen at around 10 pm in the northeastern sky. It will be directly above the head by 2 am and will stay there until dawn. In December and January, the constellation will be visible from 6 pm and will gradually disappear before the clock strikes 10 pm.

For those aiming to view the beautiful constellation from the Southern Hemisphere, during the months of July and August, Cygnus can be seen in the north-eastern sky from about 9 – 10 pm as it moves towards west throughout the night.

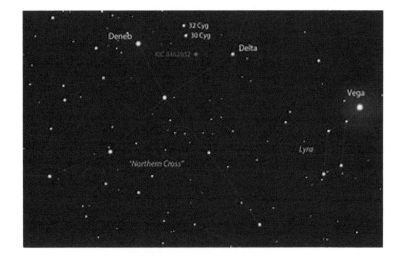

Cygnus

Legends

The Cygnus constellation is associated with several myths. The most notable of which is the legend of Cycnus and Phaeton's (mortal sun of Helios- God of Sun) friendship. The legend goes that the two friends were racing each other in the skies.

As the race got intense they flew too close to the sun and unfortunately, their chariots burned down. Both of them came crashing back to the Earth.

When Cycnus regained his consciousness, he searched around for his dear friend Phaeton and found his dead body at the bottom of the Eridanus River. As a human, he was unable to retrieve his friend's body so he made a pact with the God of Gods, Zeus. If Zeus would allow Cycnus to transform into a swan, Cycnus would live only as long as a swan usually does.

Zeus agreed to this, and Cycnus was able to gain access to his friend's dead body and give him a proper burial. By doing such, Cycnus allowed Phaeton's soul to travel to the afterlife. Zeus was touched by Cycnus' action and therefore placed him in the sky, as an image of sacrifice and friendship.

Lyra - The Harp/Lyre

To locate Lyra, look for Cygnus. It's right next door. Lyra looks like a small lopsided box or a parallelogram in the sky. It's also not far from the constellation Hercules

Lyra Constellation

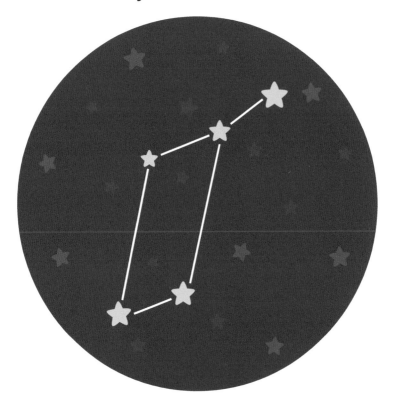

When can Lyra be seen?

In the Northern hemisphere from April to May Lyra will appear low on the horizon in the north-east around 11pm gradually moving higher in the sky before day breaks.
From June to July the constellation will appear in the east around 10 pm gradually moving higher until it is directly over head.
From August to September Lyra will appear overhead around 10 pm, slowly dipping towards the horizon in the north-west over the next few hours.
From October to December it will be visible high in the western sky between 6 and 7 pm before disappearing below the horizon several hours later.
In the Southern hemisphere Throughout July to August Lyra will appear low on the northern horizon between the hours of 8 pm to 11 pm, rising later in early winter and earlier in late winter, the constellation will stay low on the horizon moving westward for around 5 hours before dipping below the horizon

Legends

Lyra is a prominent constellation in the northern sky that is home to one of the most famous and brightest stars, Vega. The constellation represents a harp that was said to be played by the legendary Greek musician Orpheus. Orpheus was the son of Apollo and Calliope (one of the muses.) With such talented parents, it was no wonder that Orpheus was a gifted musician. The truth was, Orpheus was more than gifted. His music was magical. When he played the lyre, as his father had taught him, his songs could cast spells and soothe savage beasts.

Orpheus loved his wife, a mortal, Eurydice. When she died, he traveled down into the Underworld. He begged his great uncle Hades to allow his wife to come back to earth as herself, and not reborn as someone else.

Ever a soft touch, Hades agreed. Hades had one condition. Hades agreed to let Eurydice follow her husband back to earth and life. But, during the trip, Orpheus had to promise not to look back until both he and his wife were safely back on earth.

Orpheus was worried. He was afraid that perhaps his wife might need his help - it was a very scary trip back to the surface. He worried that perhaps Hades would not send her after all. To reassure himself that all was fine, he risked a quick look behind him, and lost his wife forever

Zodiac

There are 12 Zodiac signs, all of which can be found in the night sky. Your birthday will also fall under one of these 12 zodiac signs depending on what day and month you was born. This is where horoscopes come from. The zodiac constellations are a group of star formations that happen to cross the ecliptic line, which is the imaginary line Earth follows when it orbits around the Sun

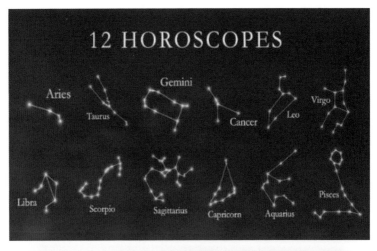

Capricorn - The Goat
Birthday - December 22nd - January 19th

Finding Capricornus To locate Capricornus, simply look for the constellation Sagittarius. It's in the southern skies for observers located north of the equator, and higher in the northern sky for folks south of the equator. Capricornus looks very much like a squashed-looking triangle.

When can Capricorn be seen?

Capricornus can be seen on the horizon starting from July at about 9pm in a south-easterly direction. As its still light, you won't be able to get such a good view of the constellation as you would later in the year. In September, when the nights are drawing in, Capricornus is fully visible in the night sky after about 9pm.
The constellation is only visible for a few months before it starts to dip below the horizon about November time.

Capricorn constellation

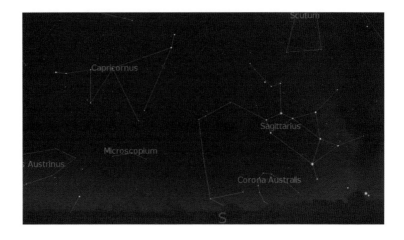

Legends

The origins of Capricorn mythology are practically unknown. The ancient Greeks had sea-goats, but there was little told about them. The Capricorn zodiac sign is often interpreted as being either a goat or a sea-goat, which is basically a creature with the front half of a goat and the tail of a fish. In actuality, both goat and sea-goat are appropriate symbols to represent Capricorn mythology. The story behind the Capricorn zodiac sign begins with the sea-goat Pricus. Pricus is the father of the race of sea-goats, who are known to be intelligent and honorable creatures who live in the sea near the shore. They can speak and think and are favored by the gods. The legend that ties Pricus to Capricorn mythology begins when the younger sea-goats, Pricus's children, find their way onto the shore. The sea-goats seem to be naturally drawn to the shore. They can use their front goat legs to pull themselves onto the beach and lay in the sun. The longer they stay on shore, though, the more they "evolve" from sea-goats into regular goats. Their fish tails become hind legs and they lose their ability to think and speak, essentially becoming the goats that we know today. This upsets Pricus a great deal.

As the father of the sea-goat race, he is determined to make sure that his children never get to the shore. If they do, he fears they will become mindless animals who can never return to sea.

After losing several of his children to the land, Pricus decides to use his ability to reverse time to force his children to return to the sea. During this time reversal, everything on earth, except Pricus, reverses itself to where it was previously, thus the goats revert back to the time to before they returned to land.

Pricus, being unaffected by the time shift, is the only one who knows what is to become of the sea-goats. He tries to warn them, even forbid them from setting foot onto the shore, but no matter what he does, or how many times he reverses time, the sea-goats eventually still find their way onto land and become regular goats.

The pivotal moment in Capricorn mythology occurs when Pricus finally realizes that he cannot control the destiny of his children, and that trying to keep them in the sea will never work, no matter how many times to tries to "start over". He resigns himself to his loneliness, and chooses to no longer reverse time, instead letting his children live their lives out to their own destiny.

In his misery, Pricus begs Chronos to let him die, as he cannot bear to be the only sea-goat left. Chronos instead allows him to live out his immortality in the sky, as the constellation Capricorn. Now he can see his children even on the highest mountain tops from the stars.

Aquarius - The Water Carrier
Birthday - January 20th - February 18th

Aquarius is visible from nearly the entire planet. It is bounded by several other constellations: Cetus (the sea monster), Pisces, Capricornus, Aquila, and Pegasus. In the Northern Hemisphere (USA, Canada, UK, and the rest of Europe), Aquarius can be found in the southern sky. On the other hand, if you are in the Southern Hemisphere, in Australia, New Zealand, or Argentina, Aquarius will be found either in the Northern sky, or directly overhead, depending on the month of the year. this is one of the hardest constellations to find with the naked eye because of its lack of recognizable features. You can find Aquarius right on the ecliptic line next to Capricorn.

Aquarius constellation

When can Aquarius been seen?

Aquarius can be found almost all year long, from April to January, but the best time to watch it in the Northern Hemisphere is between October and November when it's highest in the sky.

From mid-February to mid-March, Aquarius is directly positioned behind the Sun, making it impossible to observe it during those weeks.

When the Sun is the zodiac sign of Aquarius, from January 20 to February 19, the constellation can be really hard to locate and it might not be visible at all in some locations.

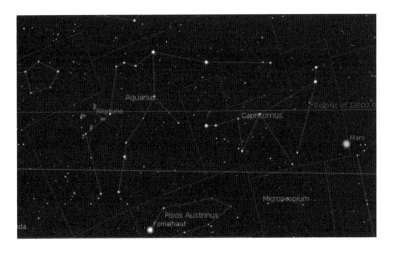

Legends

The Aquarius myth follows the story of Ganymede, a young prince, and supposedly the most beautiful young man of Troy.

One day Ganymede was off tending to his father's sheep in a grassy area on Mount Ida when he was spotted by Zeus. Zeus transformed himself into the shape of a giant eagle and swooped down from Mount Olympus to Mount Ida. He grabbed Ganymede in his talons and carried him back to Mount

Olympus to be his young servant. Now, normally in these kinds of relationships the older man would serve as a sort of mentor to the younger one, but this was Zeus, and he pretty much gets whatever he wants. So Zeus decides that Ganymede will become his personal cup-bearer, basically bringing him drinks whenever he pleases. Since Ganymede is now essentially Zeus's slave,

Zeus offers Ganymede's father a herd of the finest horses in the land as compensation for taking his son away. This apparently appeases the father, though it's doubtful that he had much of a say in the matter either way.

One day Ganymede has had enough, and he decides to pour out all of the wine, ambrosia, and water of the gods, refusing to stay Zeus's cup bearer any longer. The legend goes that the water all fell to Earth, causing inundating rains for days upon days, which created a massive flood that flooded the entire world.

At first Zeus wants to punish Ganymede, but in a rare moment of self-reflection, Zeus realizes that he has been a bit unkind to the boy, so he makes him immortal as the constellation representing the Aquarius myth.

Pisces - The Two Fish
Birthday - February 19 - March 20

While Pisces is a constellation that covers a big area, it doesn't have many bright stars. This makes it harder to find in big cities and places with high levels of light pollution. If you are in a city environment where you can't see many stars at night, using binoculars or a telescope might be necessary to find it. The most effective method to find Pisces in the sky is to find the ecliptic line. Pisces passes right through it. Pisces has two distinctive features that can be used to recognize it. Its big V shape which is one of the largest formations in the sky, and the head of the west fish, which is a group of five stars that form a circle or an irregularly shaped pentagon.

Pisces Constellation

When is Pisces visible?

The constellation Pisces is easiest to see in October and November, or on late evenings in September. Because its stars are relatively dim, Pisces is most visible in a dark country sky. Between March and May, the constellation passes behind the Sun, making it impossible for us to see it from Earth.

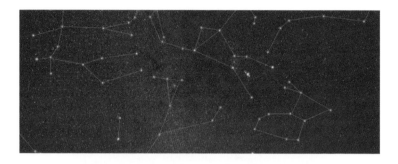

In this Greek myth, the monster Typhon descends upon Mount Olympus, threatening all of the gods and goddesses, who flee from their home (with a couple key exceptions). As Typhon approaches, the goddess Aphrodite and her son Eros (a.k.a. Venus and Cupid in Roman mythology) find themselves in need of escape.

Here's where you get to choose your own adventure. According to different versions of this legend, either Aphrodite and Eros turn into fish, two fish approach them and swim them away to safety, or they turn into fish AND two other fish take them to safety. Whichever version you prefer, truth be told, it doesn't really matter. One way or another, the two escape from Typhon thanks to two fish.

These two fish were later honored by being placed in the heavens as the constellation Pisces.

Most versions of the Typhon escape legend speak of the tails of the fish being tied together to avoid losing each other. The constellation of Pisces represents two fish with their tails tied together.

A similar version of the story is told in Syrian mythology, where two fish known as the "Ikhthyes" (or "Ichthyes") were the ones who rescued Aphrodite and Eros. Later, a different Syrian myth tells of a large and mysterious egg appearing on the Euphrates river, where two fish (or possibly men with fish-tails according to some classical art) named Aphros and Bythos who brought the egg to shore and helped it hatch. Inside the egg was Aphrodite (as her Syrian counterpart Ashtarte). Both stories have to do with some form of fish rescuing some form of Aphrodite via the river Euphrates. In both myths, the helpful fish were made into the Pisces constellation. It is believed that this legend is the reason why Syrians refused to eat fish

Aries - The Ram
Birthday - March 21st- April 19th

Aries is the figure of a ram and is visible from March to February, it is most visible in the months of November and December.
Aries is quite easy to find. Locate the Pleiades (the 5 stars close together near Orion) and Aries is just above to the right of it. Aries is not a particularly prominent constellation, so it is best to view it on a dark clear night, when it is not a full moon.

Aries Constellation

When is Aries Visible?

January - From 9pm
February - From Sunset
March 20th - April 21st -
Not Visible
May - From Sunset
June - From Sunset

July - From Sunset
August - From Sunset
September - From Sunset
October - From Sunset
November - From Sunset
December - From Sunset

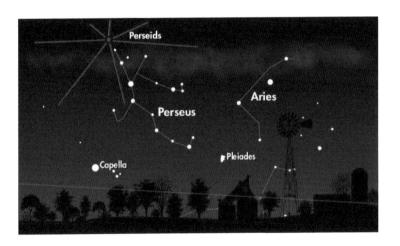

Legends

Once upon a time, there was a distant kingdom. The king of the Kingdom married another woman. However, the new queen was jealous of the king's every love for his children with the ex-wife, so she had an evil plot in her mind. The spring came and it's time to sow and farm. The new queen distributed bad wheat seeds to the farmers in the country. Of course, the seeds could not sprout no matter how they watered and fertilized. The farmers were confused. The new queen spread the rumor that the kingdom was cursed, so the wheat seeds could not sprout. She said the curse was resulted by the prince and princess's evil ideas which made the God angry, thus the punishment to the country. Quickly, the people in the country demanded the king to kill the prince and the princess to remove the curse. The king was unwilling to kill his children but he reluctantly said yes to the people's request to stop their anger. The prince and the princess's mother heard the news and she was surprised and worried, so she sought help from the great god Zeus. Zeus clearly knew it was the plot of the new queen and he agreed to offer help. On the day of the execution, a gold-hair winged ram appeared in the sky and saved the prince and the princess.

To reward this brave but careless ram, Zeus put it high in the sky, thus the Aries familiar to everyone.

Taurus - The Bull
Birthday - 20th April - 20th May

Taurus can be found right next to Orion. With Aries to the left of it.

When can Taurus be seen?

Taurus is visible for about 9 months every year, between August and April. The best months to watch it are December and January because you can find it all night long. Taurus can be seen just above Orion to the right. You can see Taurus in the Northern Hemisphere in winter and Autumn and in the Southern hemisphere Taurus can be seen from late spring and throughout the summer. In the Southern Hemisphere it will appear upside down

Taurus Constellation

Legends

This story of the Bull begins with the god, Zeus, falling in love with Europa, daughter of the King of Phoenicia. In order to get close to Europa, Zeus transformed himself into a beautiful white bull with jewel-like horns and a crescent moon on its forehead. Europa, fascinated by the beautiful and gentle bull, climbed onto the bull's back.

Once the Bull had control of the princess, he swam across the sea to the island of Crete where he changed back into his true form. Zeus and Europa had three children, and honored the bull by placing it into the sky among the stars

Legends

Castor and Pollux are the twins. They had the same Mother, but different Fathers. Pollux's father is the god Zeus (Greek mythology). As such, Pollux is an immortal while his twin brother Castor is mortal. The brother where very close, and it is said that when Castor dies, Pollux was devastated. He begged his Dad, Zeus for help. Zeus decides that rather than killing Pollux so he can be with Castor, he makes Castor immortal also, and the two of them get to live together forever as the constellation Gemini.

Gemini - The Twins
Birthday - May - 21st - June 20th

Gemini needs to be viewed on a moonless nights or in those places free of significant light pollution to be seen clearly. Gemini is right Above Orion to the left in the sky.

When can Leo be seen?

Gemini is visible in the Northern hemisphere and most of the Southern hemisphere. In the Northern hemisphere the constellation can be seen from winter to spring. In the Southern hemisphere Gemini can be seen in the summer months. The constellation will appear upside down in the Southern hemisphere.

Gemini Constellation

Cancer - The crab
Birthday - 21st June - 22nd July

The Cancer constellation is one of the trickiest zodiac constellations to find. It can be found in the sky between September and June everywhere in the world except for Antarctica. The best month to watch it is March, where it can be found directly overhead at around 9:00 PM.

During the summer months, on July and August, the constellation passes behind the Sun, which makes it impossible to see at night. You can find Cancer between Gemini and Leo. It is best to find these first, and then look for Cancer which will be in the middle of them, as the shape, size and low brightness of Cancer make it difficult to find by itself.

Cancer constellation

When is Cancer Visible?

January - From 7:30pm
February - From Sunset
March -From Sunset
April - From Sunset
May - From Sunset
June - From Sunset

July - Not visible
August - Not visible
September From 3am
October From 1am
November From 11:30pm
December From 9:30pm

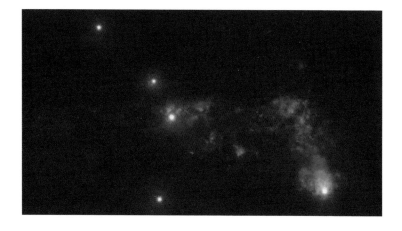

Legends

A story about Cancer is found in Greek mythology. Heracles was in a fight with the monster Hydra. A giant crab tried to help Hydra, but Heracles smashed it with his foot. The crab was so brave, that Hera put it in the sky. Can you find Cancer in the night sky?

Leo - The Lion
Birthday - July 23rd - August 22nd

Leo is just to the right to the big dipper, and just above on the right of Virgo.

When can Leo be seen?

The best time to view Leo is in April at 9pm. It is also is easily identifiable through May but can be seen from April to June.

Leo Constellation

Legends

Legend says that Leo is the Nemean lion. This lion use to catch women and take them to his lair, then when the men would come to rescue the damsel in distress, the lion would jump them and have them for his dinner. He was eventually killed by Hercules, it was the first task that he was given.

The lion also had the added advantage of possessing a skin, which was impervious to metal, stone and wood. Since Hercules could not kill the lion with any weapon, he wrestled it with his bare hands.

Virgo - The Virgin
Birthday - August 23nd - September 22nd

Using the curve of the handle, imagine a curved line, or an arc, drawn from the end of the dipper down to the bright star Arcturus (see Bootes constellation above). Then, extend that line to "drive a spike" through Spica, Virgo's brighest star. Once you've spotted Spica, you can spot the rest of the constellation. Virgo is easily visible from around the world.

Virgo constellation

When can Virgo be seen?

Virgo is only visible for about 9 months throughout the year, from November to August. and the best time to observe it and when it is the easiest to find it is in June when it is located directly overhead at around 9:00pm. To find Virgo in the evening sky, first locate the Big Dipper in the northern part of the sky. In the northern hemisphere, Virgo is most visible in the evening sky from mid-March to late June. In the southern hemisphere, it can be seen in autumn and winter.

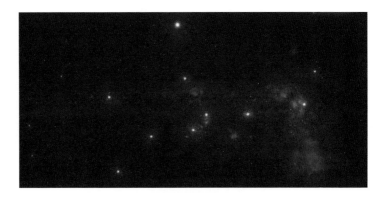

Legends

There are many legends about Virgo, one is that the constellation of Virgo is said to be Astraea, the Greek goddess of justice. Her name means 'star maiden' and she was the daughter of the Titans Astraeus (god of dusk) and Eos (goddess of dawn). According to Greek mythology, Astraea was the last immortal to abandon Earth at the end of the Silver Age. She was so disgusted by the wickedness of humans that she left to go off to the heavens and became Virgo.

Libra - The Scales
Birthday - September 23rd - October 23rd

Finding Libra is very easy. First, look for the Big Dipper. Follow the curve of the handle down to the bright star Arcturus in the nearby constellation Boötes. From there, look down to Virgo. Libra is right next to Virgo, not far from the star Spica.

Libra Constellation

When can Libra be seen?

in the Northern Hemisphere In April Libra will appear low on the south-eastern horizon around midnight, gradually moving across the southern horizon until day breaks. From May to June the constellation will be visible low in the south-eastern sky from around 10pm and dip below the south-western horizon at around 4am. In July it will appear low in the southern night sky at at around 10pm before disappearing below the south-western horizon around 3 hours later.

In the southern hemisphere in April Libra will be visible low in the eastern night sky from around 10pm, gradually moving higher before reaching overhead by around 3am. In May and June the constellation will appear in the eastern night sky at around 8pm moving higher as the night moves on, at around midnight it will begin to descend towards the western horizon. In July and August it will appear high in the northern night sky at around 8pm, heading towards the western horizon over the next few hours. In September Libra will be visible high in the western night sky from around 8pm, before disappearing below the western horizon around midnight.

Legends

Unlike the other ancient constellations Libra is not entwined with Greek mythology. In fact ancient Greeks viewed the pattern of stars as part of the adjacent constellation of Scorpius, representing the claw of the scorpion. The origins of Libra being perceived as scales goes back even further than ancient Greece, to the ancient Babylonians some 2,000 years earlier. The Babylonians associated Libra with balance and this may not have been solely down to its shape. At that time the sun would have fallen in the constellation of Libra at the autumn equinox, a time of the year between the warm and cold seasons and when day and night are of equal length.

A few thousand years later the Romans also identified the constellation as scales but not for the same reasons as suggested above. Instead the scales of Libra were associated with their God of Justice, Astraea, personified as the nearby constellation of Virgo. Libra's association with law and fairness stems from the Roman version of the constellation.

Although Libra is not entwined with Greek mythology, Because Libra represents balance and justice, harmony and equilibrium. In Greek Mythology, the Goddess of Justice is Themis. She is usually seen as a woman who is blindfolded holding the scale in her hands. She is the mother of Astraea and is sometimes seen as Libra.

Scorpio - The Scorpion
Birthday - October 23 - November 21

Antares is the brightest star in Scorpius and one of the 15 brightest stars we can see from Earth. It is one of the easiest stars to distinguish because it has a slight red color, which makes it really pop among other stars.

Thankfully, Antares is located right beside the ecliptic plane, so if you traced the imaginary line correctly, you just need to follow it until you see Antares.

Antares is right at the heart of Scorpius, so once you find it, tracing the rest of the constellation is easy. The next feature you need to recognize is the hook that makes up the "tail" of the scorpion shape. Thankfully this is also relatively easy to distinguish because the stars that form it are a lot brighter than their neighbors You can split Scorpius into 3 main parts.

- The hook that makes up the tail. This is formed by stars such as Lambda Scorpii, also known as Shaula, which is the second brightest star in the constellation.
- The core or the body of the constellation is formed by Antares right in the middle of it. Antares is also known by its scientific name, Alpha Scorpii
- The head of the scorpion is drawn by a T-shaped group of stars with Delta Scorpii (4th brightest star in the constellation) in the center as the head.

Scorpio Constellation

When can Scorpio it be seen?

Scorpius is a large and bright constellation which is mainly visible in the southern hemisphere.
In the Northern hemisphere the constellation can be seen in July and August.
In the Southern hemisphere Scorpius can be viewed from March to October.

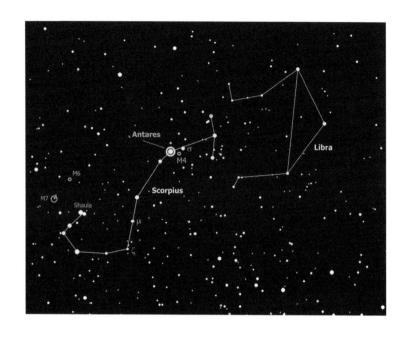

Legends

There are quite a few legends of about Scorpio, in one version Orion, the hunter, was very arrogant and he boasted to the goddess Artemis and her mother, Leto, that he would kill every animal on Earth. Artemis and Leto sent a scorpion to kill Orion.

Later, both the scorpion and Orion came to the sky and they took each other as the enemy, so they lived on opposite sides of the sky. Whenever the Scorpio rises from the east horizon, the Orion will leave from the west immediately.

Sagittarius - The Archer
Birthday - November 22 – December 21

Sagittarius the Centaur is most easily found looking South and following the Milky Way up in the Mid-Summer. On these mid-summer evenings after the sun has set, look low toward the southeast part of the sky for the classical Archer, Sagittarius. It is easiest to spot Scorpius and looking just to the left and see that Sagittarius is pointing his bow and arrow at Antares the heart of Scorpius. The most prominent feature of Sagittarius is the arrangement of the body that resembles what many point out to be a teapot. The legs of Sagittarius extend below the teapot to the South and the cape extends in the opposite direction of his bow.

When can Sagittarius be seen?

In the Northern hemisphere the constellation can be viewed low on the horizon from August to October.
In the Southern hemisphere Sagittarius can be viewed from June to November.

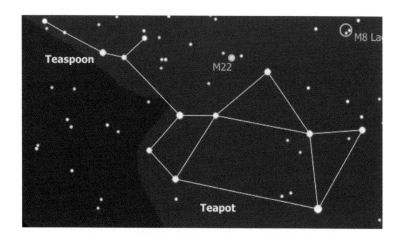

Legends

The Archer, as the constellation is called, commemorates one of the more heroic figures of the zodiac. This mythical figure is Chiron, the kindest and gentlest of the Centaurs. Centaurs were half man, half horse. Although many of them were stupid and violent, Chiron was known for his wisdom, his caring nature and his ability to teach. He was immortal; his father was Kronos and his mother was a daughter of the sea god Oceanus. Chiron tutored the young Greek heroes Achilles and Jason, among others. He was renowned among the Greeks, although he lived by himself in a cave in the countryside.

Heracles shot him with an arrow by accident. The hero had been trying to wipe out the other vicious centaurs which were plaguing the countryside. He had no intention of shooting Chiron, and was extremely remorseful. Although Chiron used his medical skills on the wound, it was incurable. Heracles' arrows were tipped with the deadly venom of the Lernean Hydra, which killed any victim it touched. But the centaur was an immortal, which changed the situation. Chiron was in terrible agony, but he could not die, although he wanted to. Prometheus the Titan saw his plight and managed to help him. It is not clear what exchange Prometheus and Chiron made, but the Titan made Chiron mortal, and enabled him to leave the Earth and go up to the heavens.

He now resides in the stars as the constellations Sagittarius.

Printed in Great Britain
by Amazon

33090462R00048